THOUGHTS, INSIGHTS,
AND
EXPERIENCES
(TIEs)

CHERRY ALDAY

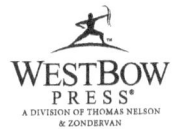

WESTBOW
PRESS®
A DIVISION OF THOMAS NELSON
& ZONDERVAN

WestBow Press books may be ordered through booksellers or by contacting:

WestBow Press
A Division of Thomas Nelson & Zondervan
1663 Liberty Drive
Bloomington, IN 47403
www.westbowpress.com
844-714-3454

ISBN: 978-1-6642-5143-4 (sc)
ISBN: 978-1-6642-5142-7 (e)

Print information available on the last page.

WestBow Press rev. date: 01/14/2022

This book is dedicated to my family – may you find this inspiring and meaningful. To the readers, enjoy reading, and thank you. God bless us all.

Proverbs 21:21 (NIV)
Whoever pursues righteousness and love
finds life, prosperity and honor.

Self &
Family

Cliché as may sound, but my family is all I have; and a godsend to me.

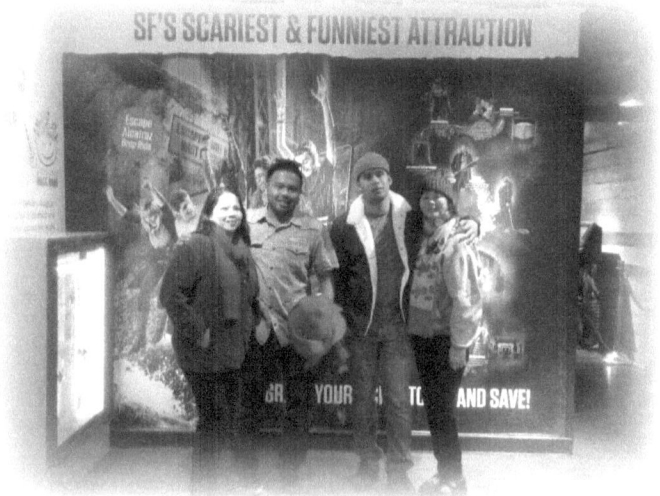

*Lyrics represent my experiences in life,
while melodies represent my emotions, and
a song is the story of my life.*

Our children are not perfect, but our responsibilities should be. There is a much greater task than providing for their needs. Provide them guidance, instill values, and teach humility.

Indeed, your love for your family is forever. Your love for others maybe forever, but boundaries are set for your own protection.

When siblings come from a different parent, what matters most is the love and care they show to each other. But the parent should never show any favoritism.

Self-reflection is good for us because sometimes our minds seem to be subconscious. It is the epitome of mindfulness, conscientiousness, and self-regard.

I learned to trust because of my loved ones and the genuine people around me.

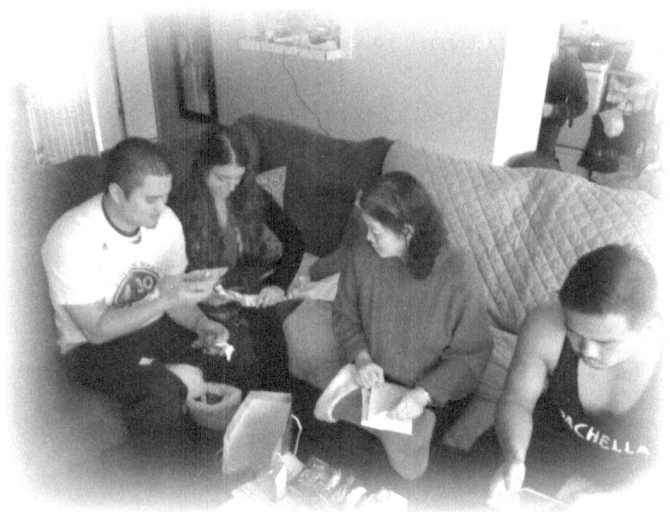

I love to take pictures simply because if my memories are gone, they will remind me of the events in my life.

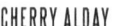
If your family cannot provide everything for you, provide something for them.

I would not have gone this far without our almighty God's path.

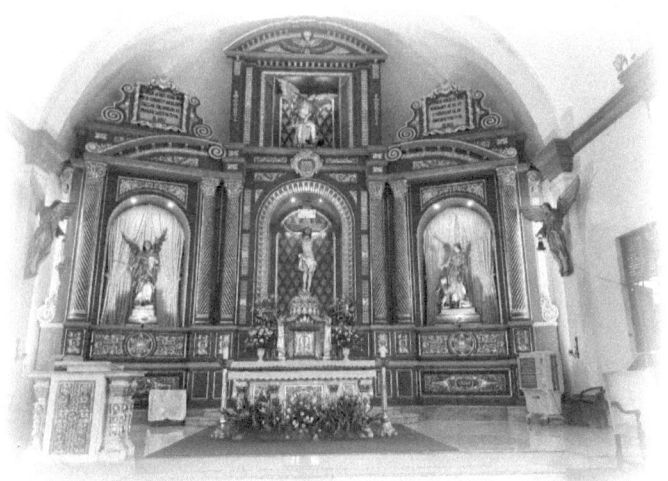

People & Relationships

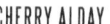

A true friend never betrays you, regardless of your distance and personal beliefs. Because once trust is broken, it might take a miracle to mend it.

People who usually do not change or are unwilling to change for the better nurture their bad habits. They don't change because of self-satisfaction, no sense of direction in life; perhaps, they simply do not care or empathize with people.

Human right is a critical aspect. People should not misuse it in any form. Sadly, some insist on this idea in their reasoning for not obeying the law. That only shows they don't know the meaning of respect.

In general, people are never satisfied with what they have because they want more and more... Contentment is a self-issue.

You don't need to convince people; your sincerity and honesty should suffice to show your true colors.

Consider outgrowing your bad habits, and maybe you'll change for a better person.

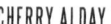

Value people for you do not know when the time comes that you don't see them anymore.

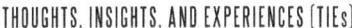
It is okay to think of our personal success.
Helping people is righteous; therefore, help
because you want to and not for benefits
or promotion.

Emotions

Falling in love brings joy to two people but hurting someone brings pain and sadness to just one.

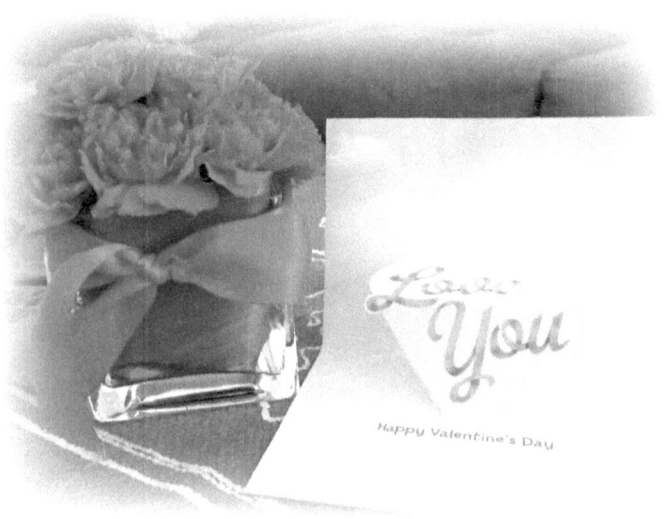

Smiles and tears can be deceiving because they may be associated with lies, truths, or both.

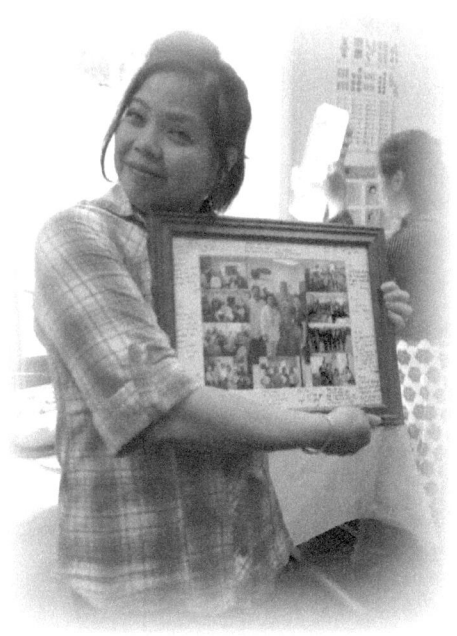

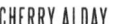

Grief is not only pain. It is a process…
a phase that no one knows when it ends.

It may not be too late to say "sorry," but the opportunity never waits.

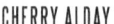
To say sorry is a way to console someone when you hurt them, but not the way to fix the problem that you have caused.

Before you advise or comfort me, look me straight in the eye and tell me… you've done me no wrong. If there's guilt in your heart, talking to me is useless.

There are two kinds of promises. One is with sincere intent, and the other one is for the sake of saying it. However, these are mere words; which one do you practice?

Some scars remain invisible that people thought you were all right.

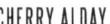

The real meaning of asking for forgiveness is not doing the same or different wrong actions.

A love that is pure and honest always gives
a person greater peace of mind.

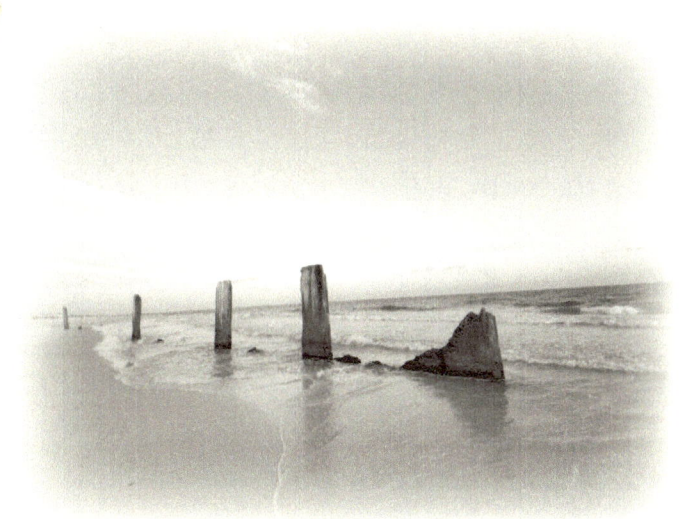

Time heals the wound, but it doesn't really cure the pain. What time does is guides us to self-reflect and figure things out.

*The concept of happiness may be
broad. Therefore, each of us may
define it differently as it requires deep
reflection before we can assert that "we're
truly happy."*

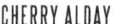
Sometimes it is better to distance yourself if you don't want to feel disappointed. Better not to display hypocrisy.

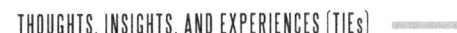
If we cannot reach out to a person due to guilt, shame, doubt, or any reason, at least include that person in our prayer.

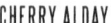
We may never forget the pain of the past.

How we cope with it is more important...

count that blessing.

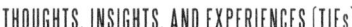

Sometimes being silent is an acceptable
or better way to deal with a situation.
However, be aware that it could also
confuse anyone or an injury to yourself.

SMILE

Saying encouraging words to someone –
makes that person smile and – illuminates
their significance. Love someone dearly
and – embrace your moments together.

The sudden death of a loved one leaves an intense pain in our hearts and souls. Not even the person himself is prepared for it. Then, we come up with too many 'whys' and realize that we should have more conversations and bonding time with that person.

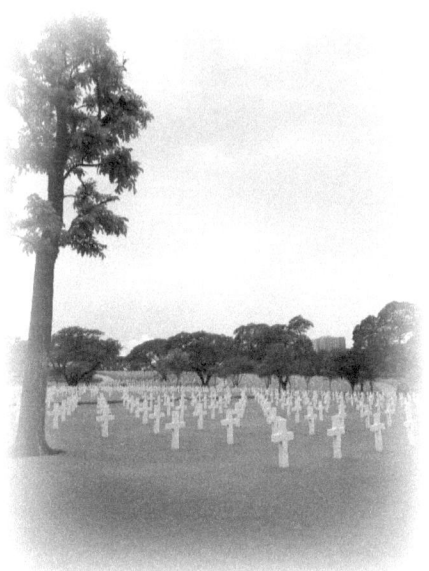

Life

Life is full of awaiting events.

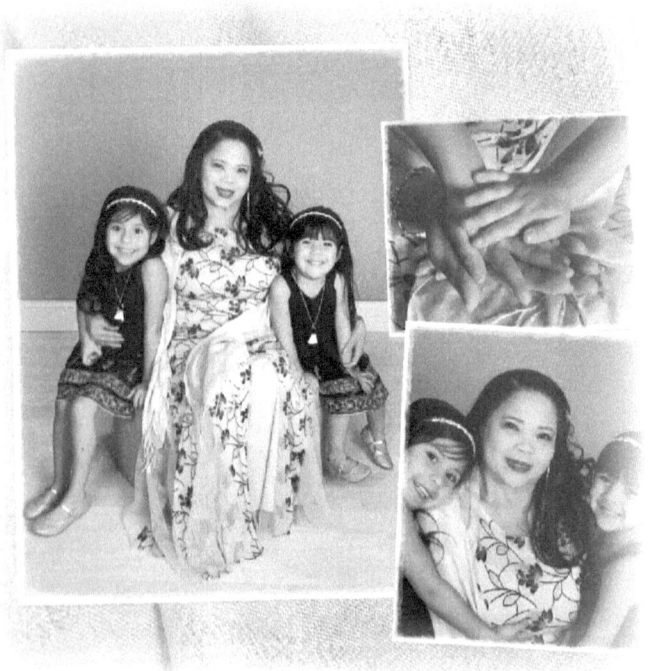

Appreciate abundance and
shun greed.

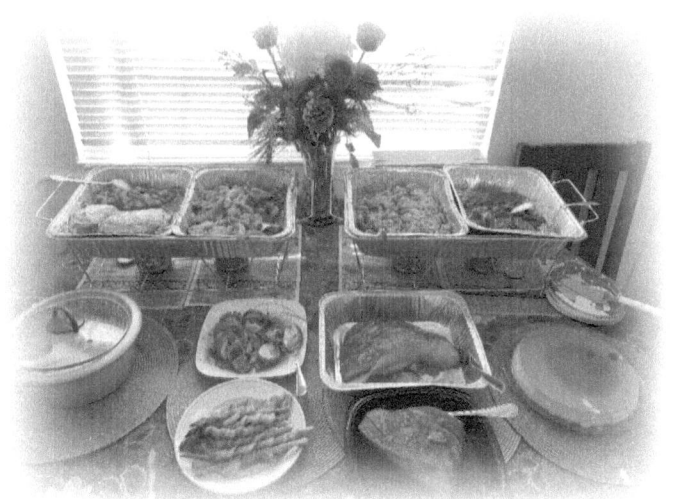

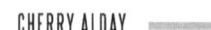
Our cultural differences do not define us. It is an opportunity to learn from each other.

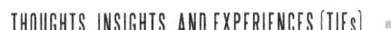

Education is not a measure of your knowledge, but rather a choice of what you want to achieve in life.

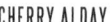
My religion may be different from yours.
We do not have to argue with each other.
Instead, be grateful that we have one.

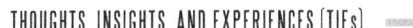

To dream big shows positivity, and acceptance is a process to consider if it's not meant for you.

Like a chapter in a book, plots may be happy and sad or good and bad. It is up to us how we make episodes in each chapter of our lives.

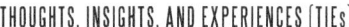

It is not about possession of material things that certainly fulfill a person, but instead taking time to internalize your values in life.

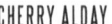
No test is perfect, just as no relationship is perfect… simply because we are not living in an ideal world.

No matter how hardworking we are,
believing in Him is still part of dealing with
life's challenges.

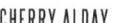

*Human lives are of utmost importance...
universally respect them, carefully nurture
them, and do not abuse the lives of others.
We are all equal in the eyes of God.*

Remember God not only in times of difficulty or failure. But also remember Him in times of success and when blessings are pouring upon you.

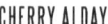

It's hard to fathom that life is sometimes not fair. Only God, the Almighty one, has the ultimate reason and explanation.

Time may not be enough to do what we want; however, finding time is something we can achieve.

Find time to be with the people you love and care for and people who genuinely care for you before it's too late. You never know when and where time will be taken away from you or them.

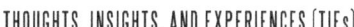
Dying is one of the saddening words we hear. We never know when our time is due. Possibly, we can ask for an extension if we desire.

About the Author

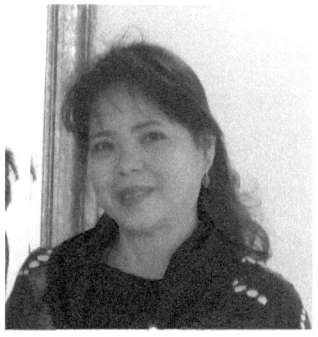

Cherry Alday was born and raised in the Philippines. She immigrated to the United States in 1995 with her son, youngest sister, and nephews. She worked in different industries and experienced working two jobs for a while. Cherry holds an MBA degree from John F. Kennedy University. Currently, she is working on her doctorate in educational leadership. Her passion for teaching leads her to foreign language education, where she teaches the Filipino language in a government institution. On a personal note, she loves to travel, watch movies, garden, do acrylic painting, and write quotes or poems.